Dear Ellen

I Talk You Talk Press

CONTENTS

I Talk You Talk Press

CHAPTER ONE

Ellen Smith sits down on the sofa in her living room. She opens a bottle of wine and pours some wine into her glass. She looks around the room. There are many boxes. She wants to unpack the boxes, but she is very tired and it is late.

My new home, she thinks.

Ellen is from Sydney. She finished university three years ago. She got a job working for a newspaper in Sydney. She is a newspaper reporter. The newspaper has an office in the central business district in Perth. Ellen's father is from Perth, so she wanted to work there for a year or two.

The boss in the Sydney office was very nice. He said, "Sure! You can work in the Perth office."

So, Ellen moved to Perth. The newspaper company found her a house in South Perth. The area is very nice and quiet. There is a park opposite the house. It is only a short walk to Swan River from the house. It is not so far from her house to the central business district. Ellen thinks, *I will be very happy here. It is a very pretty place.*

She drinks her glass of wine and decides to go to bed. She will start unpacking early tomorrow morning.

On Sunday morning, Ellen unpacks the boxes. On Sunday afternoon, the doorbell rings.

Who is that? thinks Ellen.

Ellen opens the door. There is a woman standing at the door. She is around thirty years old.

"Hi, I'm Barbara!" she says. "I live in the house next door."

"I'm Ellen. Nice to meet you."

They shake hands and talk for a while.

"If you need any help or information, just ask me," says Barbara.

"That's very kind of you, thanks," says Ellen. Barbara goes home and Ellen closes the door.

She is nice, thinks Ellen.

On Sunday evening, the house looks great.

Tomorrow, Ellen will start work at the office. She is a little nervous, but she is also excited.

I hope everyone is nice and friendly, she thinks.

It is January, so it is very hot. She can't sleep. She opens the window a little. Soon, she falls asleep.

CHAPTER TWO

Ellen gets up at 6:00am. She is still tired, but she has to get ready for work. She has egg on toast and two cups of coffee for breakfast. She puts her best suit on. The suit is grey. It is very smart. Ellen bought it in a sale in a department store in Sydney. She brushes her long blonde hair and ties it back. She puts on her make-up. She picks up her briefcase, her iPad and her handbag, and then she goes out. It is a very sunny day.

She gets into her car. The car is new. Ellen bought it last week. She starts the engine and switches the air conditioner on. She drives past the park. It is very big and green. She drives through the streets. There are some big houses. They have swimming pools and big gardens. Ellen's house doesn't have a swimming pool. It is a small house.

Ellen drives on the bridge across the river. She turns the air conditioner off, and winds the windows down. The wind from the river is very refreshing. Soon, the traffic starts to get heavier. She is in the central business district. The buildings shine in the morning sun.

"Good morning, Perth!" she says. "I hope we have a good day!" She turns the radio on and sings with the radio.

Ellen parks her car in the company car park. She looks up at the building. It is a very tall building. She takes the elevator up to the twelfth floor. She steps out of the elevator.

A man is standing next to the door. He is tall and he has red hair. He has a nice smile. He holds out his hand and says, "Hi, I'm Dean Farnham. Nice to meet you."

"Good morning, Mr Farnham," says Ellen.

"No no! Call me Dean! Everyone calls me Dean! We use first names here!"

"I see. Nice to meet you, Dean. I'm Ellen."

"Coffee?" asks Dean.

"I'd love a coffee," says Ellen.

"OK, just a moment!" says Dean.

"Are you Ellen?" asks a woman.

"Yes, I am," says Ellen. "And you are…"

"I'm Mai Kawanaka. It's good to meet you."

"You too," says Ellen.

They shake hands.

"Your desk is next to mine. Come on, I'll show you," says Mai.

Ellen and Mai sit at their desks and talk. Mai is very friendly and she talks a lot.

She introduces Ellen to the other people in the office.

"This is Regina…this is Paul….this is Lucy, and over there, in the corner, is Bill."

Ellen looks at Bill. He is sitting at his desk, looking at his computer. He has black hair and he is wearing a white shirt and a red tie. *He looks handsome,* thinks Ellen.

"Hi, Bill! I'm Ellen," she shouts.

Bill smiles. "Hi," he says quietly. "Nice to meet you."

"Bill doesn't talk very much," whispers Mai. "I think he is shy."

"Who is the boss?" asks Ellen.

"Oh, that's Tim. He is away in Melbourne this week."

"Here you are ladies. Two coffees," says Dean. He is holding two cups of coffee.

"Oh thank you, Dean," says Mai. She looks at Ellen. "Dean always makes coffee in the morning."

Dean smiles. "Always happy to be of service." He goes away.

"He seems like a nice man," says Ellen.

"Oh, he is. He's very nice," says Mai. "Everyone in the office is nice. Now, let's have coffee while I tell you about the office."

CHAPTER THREE

Ellen is enjoying her job in Perth. She is a newspaper reporter, so she has to go to many local events. She writes about the local community - the schools, hospitals, events, and concerts. It is a very interesting job.

Now, she is in the office. She looks at the calendar.

"Look, Mai. It's February twelfth. It's Valentine's Day on Saturday. Do you have a boyfriend?"

"No, I don't. I'm single. Some other people in the office are single too, so we are going to a restaurant on Hay Street for lunch and a few drinks on Valentine's Day. How about you? Do you have a boyfriend?"

"No, I don't. I came to Perth alone," says Ellen.

Dean walks over to their desks.

"Come with us on Saturday Ellen! It will be fun!" says Dean.

"Yeah, OK!" says Ellen. "Thank you for inviting me!"

"The more the merrier!" says Dean with a smile.

Ellen wakes up on Valentine's Day. Someone is knocking on her door.

Who is that? she thinks.

She gets out of bed, puts her dressing gown on, and opens the door. It is the postman.

"Ellen Smith?" he asks.

"Yes," says Ellen.

"These are for you," says the postman. The postman is holding flowers. Ellen looks at them. She is very surprised.

"What? For me? From who?"

"Read the card!" says the postman. "Have a good day!" He smiles and walks away.

"Wait!" shouts Ellen. The postman doesn't hear her. He is getting into his van. He drives away.

Ellen closes the door. She looks at the flowers. There are twelve red roses. They smell very nice. She sits down on the sofa and reads the card.

---*Dear Ellen, Happy Valentine's Day. I think of you often. Love from Bill.*---

She reads it again.

---*Dear Ellen, Happy Valentine's Day. I think of you often. Love from Bill.*---

Bill? Who's Bill? she thinks. *I only know one Bill in Perth. That's Bill in the office.*

She thinks about it. Bill is a nice man. He is very quiet and shy. Sometimes, he and Ellen have to work together. She enjoys working with Bill. He is a good worker and Ellen thinks he is handsome.

But why did he send me flowers? Is this a joke? Does he like me? This is strange, thinks Ellen. *I'm going to see him later. Should I say 'thank you'?*

Ellen looks at the roses. *They are very nice,* she thinks. *I should put them in water.*

She doesn't have a vase, so she puts some water into a saucepan and puts the roses in that. She puts the saucepan on the kitchen table.

Ellen gets ready. She puts on a long green summer dress. It is a sunny day. She is going to have some wine at lunch, so she doesn't drive to the centre of Perth. She calls a taxi.

When the taxi drives into the centre, she starts to feel nervous.

Should I tell Mai about the flowers from Bill? she asks herself. *Should I keep it a secret?*

Ellen gets out of the taxi near the restaurant on Hay Street, and pays the driver.

She walks into the restaurant. It is dark and cool. There are many couples eating lunch together.

"Ellen! Over here!" shouts Mai.

Ellen walks over to a big table in the corner. She says 'hello' to everyone. There is only one seat free. The seat is opposite Bill. She sits down and smiles nervously at Bill. Everyone orders wine, pasta, salad and pizza.

After a few bottles of wine, everyone is relaxed.

"So," says Dean. "Did anyone get anything for Valentine's Day? Any cards? Any flowers? Chocolates?"

"I didn't," says Mai. "I never get anything."

"Aw, that's too bad," says Paul, laughing. "Next year, I'll buy you some chocolates."

"You are too kind!" says Mai. "But really, you know, I should buy you chocolates."

"Me? Why?" asks Paul.

"Well, in Japan on Valentine's Day, the women give chocolates to men. We have to give chocolate to the men in our office."

"Really?" says Paul. "So why didn't you give me chocolates? You must give me chocolates on Monday morning Mai!"

"Too late!" says Mai.

Everyone laughs.

"How about you Ellen?" asks Paul. "Did you get anything for Valentine's Day?"

Everyone looks at Ellen. She has drunk a lot of red wine. She looks at Bill.

"Ask Bill," she says.

"What?" says Paul.

"Ask Bill," says Ellen again.

Everyone looks at Bill. Bill looks shocked. "Why ask me?" he asks.

"Yeah Ellen, why ask Bill?" asks Dean.

"Well, the postman woke me up at 8:00am. I was not happy about that," says Ellen.

"What did he bring?" asks Dean.

"The flowers," says Ellen.

"What flowers?" asks Paul.

"The flowers!" says Ellen. "The flowers from Bill."

Everyone looks at Bill.

"Huh? What?" asks Bill. "I don't...."

"And you think about me often, right?" says Ellen, smiling.

"What?" asks Bill. His face is red. Everyone is looking at him.

"Ellen? Are you OK?" asks Mai.

"I'm OK. Are the flowers a joke, Bill? The flowers! You sent them!" says Ellen.

"I'm sorry Ellen. I...I..." Bill cannot speak. Everyone is looking at him.

Dean looks at Bill and says, "So, you are sending flowers to the new girl! You don't waste time!"

"But I…I…" says Bill. "I didn't send you any flowers, Ellen!"

Mai looks at Bill. He looks very upset. "OK everyone. Let's talk about something else," she says.

Everyone starts to talk about work. Ellen is very quiet. She is thinking about the flowers. She watches Bill.

Why did he say 'I didn't send you any flowers'? thinks Ellen. *Maybe he is shy. I told everyone about the flowers. That was a bad idea. I drank too much wine.*

"Time to go to a bar!" says Dean. Everyone stands up.

"Ellen, are you coming?" asks Mai.

"No, I'm going home," says Ellen. "I have many things to do tomorrow."

Ellen goes home. She has a headache. She goes to bed but she can't sleep. She is thinking about the afternoon, the flowers, and Bill.

CHAPTER FOUR

On Monday, Ellen goes to the office. Bill is sitting at his desk.

"Hi Bill," says Ellen.

"Hi," says Bill quietly. He doesn't look at Ellen.

I think he is upset, thinks Ellen. *He is upset because I told everyone about the flowers.*

"Hi Ellen," says Mai. "Ellen, what were you talking about on Saturday? What flowers? Did Bill send you flowers?"

Ellen tells Mai about the flowers. Mai listens very carefully.

Then, she says to Ellen, "He likes you. He was shocked because he is shy. Because you said, 'Bill sent me flowers'. Now, everyone knows. Do you like him?"

"I don't know," says Ellen. "Of course, I think he is a nice man. I think he is handsome. And I like quiet men. But...do I want to date him? I don't know. I don't know him very well. The flowers and the card were...I don't know...they were a little..."

"A little strange for you?"

"Yeah, a little strange," says Ellen.

"Well, Bill isn't a bad man," says Mai. "I think he is just shy. He wanted to tell you his true feelings. So, he sent you some flowers. That's nice. But you drank too much wine and told everyone in the office. That was not good, Ellen."

"I know," says Ellen. "I feel bad. I must say 'sorry' to Bill."

A few weeks later, Ellen comes home from work. There is a letter in the post box. She looks at the handwriting.

It's the same handwriting! she thinks. She opens it and reads it.

---*Dear Ellen, I hope you liked the flowers. I never hear from you. But I am still waiting. I sit in the café near ABC Supermarket every Friday at 12:00 waiting for you. But you never come. Maybe you don't want to see me. But I will wait. I will wait until I die. Love from Bill.*---

There is no return address on the envelope. Ellen thinks about it. *This is really strange. I have to talk to Bill tomorrow.*

The next day, Ellen goes to work early. She is alone. She waits for Bill. He is usually very early. She hears the elevator doors.

This is him! she thinks.

Bill walks into the office. He looks surprised.

"Good morning, Ellen," he says.

"Good morning Bill. Bill, if you want to talk to me, it's OK. You can talk to me. You don't have to send me letters."

"Pardon?" says Bill.

"You don't have to send me letters Bill! You can talk to me! If you want to see me on Friday at the café, you can ask me!"

Bill looks at her. "Ellen, what are you talking about? I didn't send you any letters."

"Why are you lying to me?" asks Ellen.

Mai walks into the office. "Good morn… oh, sorry…is everything OK?"

She looks at Ellen and then at Bill.

"Yes, I'm fine Mai, but Ellen seems to have problems," says Bill. He walks over to his computer and starts to work. He doesn't look at Mai or Ellen.

Ellen and Mai sit down at their desks.

"What was that about?" asks Mai.

Ellen tells Mai about the letter. "I don't like it, Mai. He is waiting for me. He is waiting every Friday in the café until he dies! It's really strange!"

"Bring me the letter tomorrow," says Mai. "I want to see it. If Bill is sending you strange letters, you should talk to the boss."

"Yes, I think so too," says Ellen.

The next day, Ellen shows Mai the letter.

"This is not Bill's handwriting. This is not from Bill," says Mai, shaking her head.

"But if Bill didn't send the flowers and the letter, who did? No one knows me in Perth."

"Was there a return address on the envelope?" asks Mai.

"No, nothing," says Ellen. "I don't like it. Someone knows my name and my address. It has to be Bill! If it isn't Bill, it is a stranger!"

"Maybe it's one of your neighbours?" says Mai.

"Maybe," says Ellen. "Should I go to the police?"

"I don't think the police will help you. I have a better idea. Let's go to the café on Friday. Let's go together!"

"Are you sure?" says Ellen. "It might be dangerous."

"We'll be OK! It's lunchtime in a café near a big supermarket. There will be many people. Let's have lunch at the café."

In the evening, Ellen goes home. When she opens the door, she looks at the park opposite.

Is someone in the park? Is someone watching me? she thinks.

She goes into her house and locks the door.

CHAPTER FIVE

Ellen feels nervous on Friday morning. She has to write a story about a local school, but she cannot think very well.

"Are you OK?" asks Mai.

"Yes, I am. But I'm a little nervous," says Ellen.

"I'm a little nervous too," says Mai. "I hope he is cute!"

"Mai! Stop it!" says Ellen.

"Oh come on, Ellen. A man sends you flowers! He wants to meet you! It's romantic!" says Mai.

"Mai, be quiet!" says Ellen.

At 11:30, Mai and Ellen drive to the other side of the city. They park in the supermarket car park and walk to the café. There are many people in the café having lunch. They sit at a table at the back of the café, and watch the other people.

"We are looking for a man," says Ellen. "A man alone."

They look around. There is a workman eating an egg sandwich and reading a newspaper. There is a businessman looking at his iPad. There are some women talking. There is a couple in the corner. They are looking out of the window. There is an old man. He is drinking a cup of tea. He is also looking out of the window.

After ten minutes, the workman stands up and goes. Then, at 12:45, the business man goes. Only the women and the old man stay in café.

"Ellen, we have to go back to the office," says Mai. "I don't think he is here."

"Yes, it's getting late. Maybe he is outside, watching us. Maybe he is sitting in his car. I don't like this," says Ellen.

They stand up. They walk past the old man's table. He looks at them. Then, he looks out of the window again.

Ellen and Mai go back to the office. Ellen tries to work, but she can't stop thinking about the café and the people in the café.

Maybe the man didn't go to the café? Maybe he was busy? she thinks.

She decides to go again next Friday.

Back at the office, Ellen watches Bill. He is at the photocopier making copies of a report. She wants to say 'sorry', but it is difficult. Now, he never talks to her.

All week, Ellen waits for Friday. She tries to talk to Bill, but he doesn't talk to her. She doesn't get any more letters. She works hard and tries to forget about Friday.

CHAPTER SIX

It's Friday. Ellen and Mai go to the café again. They sit at the same table. They watch everyone coming into the café.

"The same people are here," says Mai. "Maybe they come here for lunch every day."

Ellen looks around. She sees the businessman looking at his iPad. There are two workmen eating quickly. Some women are drinking tea and talking loudly. The old man in the corner is looking out of the window. There is a couple with young children too. The children are very noisy.

"What should we do?" asks Ellen.

Mai thinks for a minute. Then, she says, "I have an idea."

"What?" says Ellen.

"Shout the name 'Bill' very loudly," says Mai.

"People will look at us!" says Ellen.

"No, only Bill will look at you!" says Mai.

"OK," says Ellen. She puts her coffee down. "BILL!" she shouts.

They look at the other people. A child looks at them. The old man looks at them. He looks at them for a long time. Then, he looks out of the window again.

"He's not here," says Mai. "Come on, it's getting late. Let's go back."

They stand up. When they walk past the old man's table, he looks at Ellen. She looks at him. Then, she walks out of the café.

In the afternoon, Ellen thinks about the old man. He looked at her for a long time.

But why? thinks Ellen. *Maybe his name is Bill...Is it the old man? No...but...*

She turns to Mai.

"Mai, who lived in the house before me?"

"I don't know. The newspaper company found it two weeks before you came here. I think it was empty for a long time."

"Which real estate agent manages the house?"

"Burt's Happy Housing I think," says Mai. "Why?"

"I have an idea," says Ellen.

CHAPTER SEVEN

After work, Ellen goes to Burt's Happy Housing. A man is sitting behind a desk.

"Good day. I'm Burt. Can I help you?"

"Yes," says Ellen. "I live at number 5 Park Gardens. Could you tell me who lived there before me?"

"I'm sorry, that's private information," says Burt. "Why do you want to know?"

"Well, someone sent flowers and a letter. But I don't think they are for me."

"What name was on the letter?"

"Ellen Smith."

"And what's your name?"

"Ellen Smith."

Burt laughs. "So they are for you!"

"I don't know…" says Ellen.

"Well, Burt's Happy Housing started managing the house last year. A couple lived in it. Their name was not Smith."

"OK, thanks," says Ellen. She walks out into the car park.

OK, Burt won't tell me, but maybe the neighbours will, she thinks. She gets into her car and drives home.

Ellen parks her car next to her house and walks to Barbara's house. Barbara's car is outside the house. She is home from work.

She knocks on the door. Barbara opens it.

"Hi Ellen, how is everything?" says Barbara.

"Good thanks. Barbara, I have a question for you. Who lived in the house before me?"

"A young couple lived there. I don't know who lived there before the young couple. When I moved to this area, they were living in the house."

"When did they leave?" asks Ellen.

"They moved out about two months before you moved in."

"Do you know them? Do you have a telephone number or address for them?"

"Why? Is there a problem?" asks Barbara.

"No, there's no problem. I'd like to talk to them about the house. That's all," says Ellen.

"Well, they were very nice and we became friends. I have their address."

"I'd like to talk to them. I'd like to see them on Sunday. Could you call them for me, please?"

"Sure," says Barbara.

"Thanks Barbara," says Ellen.

Later, Barbara calls Ellen. "They will be home on Sunday. Here is their address."

Ellen writes the address on a notepad.

She switches on her computer and looks for the house on Google Earth. It is in East Perth.

I will go there on Sunday, she thinks.

CHAPTER EIGHT

On Sunday, Ellen drives to East Perth. She gets there at 11:00am. She has lunch in a restaurant. It is very hot outside. She has to wait until 1:00pm for the meeting.

She walks along the riverside. There are many people walking. They are enjoying the sun. She looks out at the river. The water is deep blue. It is the same colour as the sky. *This is a beautiful place,* she thinks. *I'm glad I moved to Western Australia.*

At 1:00pm, Ellen drives to the house. The street is very quiet. The house is bigger than Ellen's house. It looks new. It has a small garden at the front.

She knocks on the door.

"Hello!" says a woman. She opens the door.

"Hi, I'm Ellen."

"Hi, Ellen, I'm Charlotte. Come in!"

Ellen walks in to the house.

"My husband is out shopping. He will be home soon," says Charlotte. She makes some lemonade in the kitchen. Ellen looks around. The living room is cool. The walls are white and there are modern art pictures on the walls.

"Take a seat, Ellen."

"Thanks," says Ellen. She sits down on the black leather sofa.

"So, how can I help you?" says Charlotte.

"Who lived in the house before you?" asks Ellen.

"Oh, let me see…it was a long time ago…" Charlotte closes her eyes. "It was an old woman. Her name was Ellen. The same as you!"

"Really? What was her last name?" asks Ellen.

"Oh I'm not sure. Let me see…. it was…hmm…I can't remember…hmm…oh, who was it!?"

"Hi, I'm home!"

"Ah, this is my husband, Jake," says Charlotte. "Jake, come in here! Ellen is here!"

Jake comes into the living room and sits down.

"What was the last name of the old woman, Jake? The old woman in our old house."

"It was Smith," says Jake.

"Ellen Smith!?" says Ellen. "I'm Ellen Smith!"

"That's funny!" says Charlotte laughing. "Why do you want to know about the old woman?"

"Well, on Valentine's Day, I got twelve red roses," says Ellen.

"Lucky you!" says Charlotte.

"No, I'm not lucky. No one knows me in Perth. I thought, 'Maybe the roses were for someone else'. I think they were a present for Ellen!"

"Yeah, Charlotte, do you remember?" says Jake. "Twelve red roses came to the house on Valentine's Day last year. I was angry. I thought, 'Charlotte has a boyfriend'! But I looked at the card. The card said, 'Dear Ellen…' so the flowers were for the old woman."

"Yes, that's right! I remember now! It was so cute. And after that, we got a letter. A letter addressed to Ellen Smith. But we didn't open it. It was not our letter."

"I got a letter too. But, I opened it," says Ellen. "That was bad of me."

"No, it wasn't bad of you. Your name is the same! You thought the letter was for you!" says Jake.

"Where did the old woman go?" asks Ellen.

"I don't know. She was very old. About eighty. I think she went into an old people's home. Maybe she died already. I don't know. Why? Do you want to find her?"

"Yes, I do," says Ellen. "I think a man sent the flowers. I think I know him. He is a very old man."

"I hope you find her. The man is very romantic. They will be very happy," says Charlotte.

"I hope so too," says Ellen. She stands up. "It's getting late. I have to go now. Thank you for your help."

"If you get any information, let us know," says Charlotte. "It will be a very nice story!"

Ellen gets into her car and drives home.

CHAPTER NINE

It is Monday morning. Ellen goes to work.

"Hi Ellen," says Mai. "How was your weekend?"

"It was good, thanks. How was yours?"

"Not bad. I met some friends, went shopping…"

"Mai, I need to talk to you about something," says Ellen.

Ellen tells Mai the story about the man, Charlotte and Jake.

"I want to call the local old people's homes, because I want to find old Ellen," says Ellen. "But they will not give me any private information."

Mai thinks for a minute. "I have an idea. Bill's sister works in an old people's home. Talk to Bill. I think he can help you."

Ellen thinks, *I must say 'sorry' to Bill. The flowers were not from him. The flowers were not for me. The flowers were from old Bill. They were for old Ellen.*

Ellen walks over to Bill.

"Bill, do you have time to talk?"

Bill looks up from his computer. "Yes," he says.

"First, I have to say 'sorry' to you. I know you didn't send me the flowers…I…I thought you sent them, and I drank a lot of wine in the restaurant on Valentine's Day, and I'm really sorry…but the woman has my name and the man is old, old Bill, not you and…"

Bill holds up his hands. "Ellen! Stop! I don't understand you! What are you talking about? Sit down, relax, and tell me your story."

Ellen sits down next to Bill.

She tells him the story. She tells him about the flowers and the card, and the old man in the café. He listens very carefully. Then, he says, "I'll call my sister. Let's try to arrange something."

A few hours later, Bill walks over to Ellen's desk.

"I spoke to my sister, Pauline. Ellen is not in Pauline's old people's home. So, she called her friend, Sandy. Sandy works in a different old people's home. There is no Ellen Smith in Sandy's home. So Sandy called two more homes. There is an Ellen Smith in one of the homes. The home is outside Perth city centre. I have a plan. Are you free on Friday lunch time?"

"Yes, of course," says Ellen.

"Good," says Bill. "This is the plan…"

CHAPTER TEN

It is Friday lunchtime. Ellen and Bill are in the café near the supermarket. Old Bill is also in the café. He is sitting at the table next to the window. He is drinking a cup of tea and looking out of the window at the car park.

An old woman and a young nurse come into the café. They sit at a table near the door. The old woman walks with a stick. She cannot walk very well. She is wearing a red dress and ear rings. Her grey hair is tied back and she is wearing a large red hairclip. She is wearing bright red lipstick. Ellen thinks that she looks very pretty.

The nurse looks at Ellen and Bill and smiles. They smile at the nurse. Then, Ellen walks over to the old man.

"Excuse me, Bill?" she says.

The old man looks at her. He is very surprised.

"Yes?" he says.

"There is someone here to see you," says Ellen.

"Who are you?"

"I'll tell you later. Could you come over here please?"

"I'm drinking my tea," says the old man.

"I'm sorry, but it's very important. A lady wants to meet you."

"A lady? Oh, I can't keep a lady waiting," says the old man.

Ellen smiles. "No, you can't! So, please come with me!"

The old man stands up slowly. Ellen holds his arm. "This way," she says.

She takes the man over to old Ellen's table.

"Oh!" he says.

Old Ellen turns around. "Bill!" she says. "Bill!"

"Ellen! You came!" says the old man. Ellen looks at him. There are tears in his eyes. "I waited for you for a long time."

Old Bill sits down at the table next to old Ellen.

"Did you like the flowers?" he asks.

Old Ellen doesn't understand. "Flowers? What flowers?"

Bill walks over to the table. "I think he means these," he says. Bill has a bunch of twelve red roses. He gives the roses to old Bill. "Here, give these to Ellen," says Bill.

Old Bill smiles and takes the roses. "Thank you, young man," he says. He gives them to old Ellen. She looks at them and smells them.

"Oh they are beautiful!" she says. "Beautiful!" Then she looks at Bill. "But who are you?" Then she looks at Ellen. "And who are you?"

Ellen and Bill sit down. They tell old Bill and Ellen the story.

"That's right," says old Ellen. "When I met Bill at bingo, I thought, 'He's a very nice man.' We talked a lot about many things. We met here, in the café every Friday. One day, I gave him my address. After that, I became sick. I was in hospital for a long time. Then, I couldn't live alone. So, I went into an old people's home."

"Every Valentine's Day, I sent you flowers," says old Bill. "And every Friday, I came here. I waited for you."

"This is a very nice story," says Ellen. "Can we put it in the newspaper?"

"Of course," says old Ellen. "But do you have a mirror? I want to check my make-up before you take my photograph."

"You don't need to check your make-up. You look beautiful," says old Bill.

Old Ellen looks at Ellen. "Men!" she says, shaking her head. "Someone bring me a mirror."

Bill takes some photographs and everyone talks together.

Ellen looks at her watch. "Bill, it's nearly one o'clock. We have to go back to the office."

They leave the café. Old Bill and old Ellen are talking to each other.

"I think they will talk for hours," says Ellen, laughing. "I think old Ellen's nurse will be very tired!"

"Yes," says Bill. "It's a wonderful story. I'm happy we could help them. Hey, we didn't eat anything. Are you hungry?"

"Yes, I am," says Ellen.

"Let's get a hamburger on the way back to the office," says Bill.

"Bill, what are you doing later?" asks Ellen.

"I have no plans. Why?" says Bill.

"Would you like to go out to dinner with me?" asks Ellen. "I want to say 'sorry'. And I'd like to talk to you more. We never talk in the office."

Bill smiles at Ellen. "Yes, I'd love to!"

"Great!" says Ellen. "Ellen and Bill can celebrate helping Ellen and Bill!"

CHAPTER ELEVEN

The next day, Mai and Ellen are looking at the newspaper. On the front page, there is a big story about Ellen and Bill, and old Ellen and Bill. In the photograph, everyone looks very happy.

"It's a great story," says Mai. "The old woman is called Ellen Smith. You are called Ellen Smith. The old man is called Bill. Our Bill is called Bill. It's unbelievable. On our online newspaper site, many people are writing comments. The comments say, "Young Ellen and young Bill should be a couple, too!""

Ellen laughs.

"But Ellen, I think it's a great idea. You and Bill look really good together," says Mai.

"Really?" asks Ellen.

"Yes. And you went on a date last night, right?"

"Er, we went out for dinner, Mai," says Ellen. "That's all. It was only dinner. Not a date."

"Dinner is not a date?" asks Mai.

"No! Well, maybe," says Ellen.

"No flowers?"

"Well…er…"

"He gave you flowers, right?"

"How do you know?" asks Ellen.

"I saw you last night. I was in a bar across the road from the taxi stand. You were getting in a taxi. You were holding a bunch of red roses," says Mai.

"You saw me? Were you following me?" says Ellen.

"No, I was just in a bar! But, now I understand. Bill was upset in the restaurant on Valentine's Day because he liked you. He wanted to be your boyfriend."

"We talked about that," says Ellen. "There is no problem now."

"So, are there two couples in Perth called Ellen and Bill now?" asks Mai.

"Maybe," says Ellen smiling. "Maybe!"

THANK YOU

Thank you for reading Dear Ellen. (Word count: 5,798) We hope you enjoyed Ellen's story.

There are quizzes about this book on our free study site I Talk You Talk Press EXTRA. http://italk-youtalk.com

If you would like to read more graded readers, please visit our website http://www.italkyoutalk.com

Other Level 1 graded readers include
A Business Trip to New York
A Homestay in Auckland
A Trip to London
Haruna's Story Part 1
Haruna's Story Part 2
Haruna's Story Part 3
Ken's Story Part 1
Ken's Story Part 2
Life is Surprising!
Strange Stories
The Christmas Present
The Old Hospital
We Met Online

ABOUT THE AUTHOR

I Talk You Talk Press is a Japan-based publisher of language textbooks, graded readers and language learning/teaching resources.

Our team is made up of highly experienced language teachers and translators, who have all studied at least one additional language to an advanced level.

This experience enables us to design our materials from the perspective of both the teacher and the learner. We consult with both teachers and language learners when designing our textbooks and graded readers, and test our materials extensively in the classroom before publication.

We are a fast-growing press, and currently publish graded readers for learners of English. We publish new graded readers monthly.

www.ingramcontent.com/pod-product-compliance
Lightning Source LLC
Chambersburg PA
CBHW022350040426
42449CB00006B/813